THE
WORKPLACE POLIT[...]
POCKETBOO[...]

By David Bancroft-Turner

Drawings by Phil Hailstone

"This pocketbook helps you navigate through a [...] subject by providing practical and action-orientated advice. I will certai[...] [...] using it to improve my own effectiveness within my organisation."
Eleni Nicholas, Group Managing Director UK & Ireland, The Nielsen Company

"I know from work that Dave has done with us over the last couple of years that he is a leading authority on workplace and organisational politics. This book provides a very practical insight into how people behave within organisations and suggestions on how to positively influence your working environment."
Mike Edwards, HR Manager, Management Development, Lloyds TSB

Published by:
Management Pocketbooks Ltd
Laurel House, Station Approach, Alresford, Hants SO24 9JH, U.K.
Tel: +44 (0)1962 735573   Fax: +44 (0)1962 733637
E-mail: sales@pocketbook.co.uk
Website: www.pocketbook.co.uk

This edition published 2008

British Library Cataloguing-in-Publication Data.   A catalogue record for this book is available from the British Library.

ISBN 978 1 903776 90 2

Design, typesetting and graphics by **efex ltd**. Printed in U.K.

INTRODUCTION

A FACT OF LIFE...

Workplace politics has always existed where groups of people have decided to work or live together. However much you would like to wish it away, its impact and effects are unlikely to disappear.

In fact if you go back to some of the earliest manuscripts, written by our ancestors, you will see examples of politics in the family, at work and in social settings.

It appears on numerous occasions in the works of Shakespeare. Nowadays newspapers are full of stories of political intrigue.

This is a subject that is here to stay.

POLITICS WITH A SMALL *'p'*

This book is focused on politics with a small 'p' – what happens in the workplace, be it public, private or voluntary sector, big or small – not what happens in Governments or Parliaments where politicians argue, speak in spin, manipulate others for their own benefit and stab each other in the back. On the other hand you may say this is exactly what happens in your organisation!

Workplace politics suffers from bad press – it is linked in many people's minds to the behaviour of unscrupulous politicians, and as a result it is usually talked about in the negative. In organisations over 80% of people believe it is linked in some way to **behaviour without integrity**. Reading on will show you how you can make it a positive.

INTRODUCTION

WHAT IS WORKPLACE POLITICS?

Some definitions:

- Achieving results by using the informal as well as the formal channels
- The achievement of organisational and/or personal goals by using appropriate skills and strategies
- The covert, rather than the overt, way of getting things done
- The way in which things are done around here
- The ability to understand others and to influence them to achieve my and/or the organisation's objectives
- People playing games I don't like or understand
- People using power I don't have or in a way I don't like
- Your interpretation of other people's behaviour (what they say and do)

Which ones do you agree with?

SOME COMMON POLITICAL SITUATIONS

SCENARIO ONE – A COMMON TALE OF EMAIL ABUSE

A colleague from another department has asked you for some information. Their deadline has only just passed and you receive the email below. (You genuinely forgot to respond as you have been busy with, for you, more important work.)

'I called you last week to get information on the Rivers account. You have as yet not responded to me and my client has called me to complain that their needs have not been met. They are really angry.'

As you are reading the email you notice it has been copied to your manager and the sender's manager. What do you now do?

Some questions for you to consider:

- Why did your colleague cc the email?
- Why haven't the two managers responded to either of you?
- Why has your colleague sent an email rather than phone you about it?
- What sort of mood was your colleague in when the email was sent?
- What sort of mood are you in, right now?

SOME COMMON POLITICAL SITUATIONS
SCENARIO TWO – THE CLOSED DOOR

You have applied for a promotion in your organisation. You really want this new job. Your boss calls you in to tell you that you have not got it. They add: 'Please do not ask any further questions about why you have not been successful. The director responsible has asked me to tell you that you should not speak to anybody about this and that you should wait for the next opportunity.' What do you do?

Some questions for you to consider:

● Why the secrecy?

● What is your boss really telling you?

● When is the next opportunity?

● Why did the director tell your boss and not you?

● How can you find out what is really going on and who can you ask?

SOME COMMON POLITICAL SITUATIONS

SCENARIO THREE – THE GOAL DIFFERENCE

You have been asked to sell some company assets by the end of the year. Both you and your manager have this written into your objectives. You have a buyer but another party has indicated that if you can wait until the first part of next year they will pay twice the rate you have been offered. You speak to your boss who says: 'Sell it now; I'm not interested in next year.' What do you do?

Some questions for you to consider:

- Is this battle worth fighting?
- If the company is going to suffer financially, what are your options?
- Are you prepared to go over your manager's head?
- Why isn't your boss interested?
- What is their real agenda?

SOME COMMON POLITICAL SITUATIONS
SCENARIO FOUR – ROCK AND A HARD PLACE

Your functional boss, based abroad in a global head office function, has asked you to implement in your organisation a new process that you know your local CEO (to whom you also report) does not support. You are expected to make a presentation to the CEO next week recommending the new process. Ouch – what do you do?

Some questions for you to consider:

● Why doesn't your superior connect with your CEO?

● What are the agendas going on here?

● What could you do before the presentation?

● Who else is interested in this situation?

● Why a presentation?

CHOOSE TO DO SOMETHING!

All four of these scenarios are typical of the different, and difficult, political situations that many people face on a daily basis. The key is that doing nothing is not really an option and, if chosen, can be high risk.

Depending on the type of political animal you are (and believe me, you are one!) you may take one course of action while another person will take another. It is not a question of right or wrong, it is about the implications of your action.

How will it be seen by others and what conclusions will they come to about you? And how might that perception alter their behaviour towards you in the future?

Later in the book we will investigate the different types of actions you could take. You always have a choice...

INTRODUCTION

BAD NEWS AND GOOD NEWS

Negative political manoeuvring has been cited as the number one cause of stress in the workplace.

The negative effects of workplace politics are estimated to cost the UK economy £7.8 billion per annum.

It can adversely affect morale, productivity, customer service and effective team working.

In a recent report 69% of respondents stated that political behaviour was very common – and on the increase.

The good news is that with a higher level of political intelligence, you can use a distinct set of skills and behaviours to make your organisation more politically positive, more productive and improve the working environment for all concerned.

Everybody wins!

YOU MAY ASK...

So why do I need to manage workplace politics?

If you don't, you run the risk of being a victim of other people's behaviour. We are not asking you to be negative, sneaky, difficult or Machiavellian, we are asking you to think about using a set of skills that will be good for you **and** the organisation.

Why can't I just ignore it?

You can! And many people do. What then happens is they complain that they cannot get things done and do not understand how the organisation really works. With a small amount of work and preparation and a few changes to the things that you do, you will be able to be more effective and in turn make your organisation a better place in which to work, achieve your objectives **and** those of the organisation.

WHERE WILL YOU FIND POLITICS?

- In the workplace
- In the home
- With your friends
- With your neighbours
- In your hobby classes
- In your school
- In the café
- In the hairdresser
- With your boss
- With your partner

Everywhere!

WHAT'S YOUR PERCEPTION?

Some words you may associate with organisational politics:

Manipulation	Back stabbing	Stolen ideas
Blame	Machiavellian	Influence
Power	String pulling	Game playing
Coercion	Gossiping	Buck passing
Working with allies	Getting things done	Cliques
Being clever	Bypassing bureaucracy	Networking effectively

Which ones do you agree with?

Many of the words could be interpreted as negative. Some, however, are positive and many could be positive if you were to think of them slightly differently. If, for instance, you were to present your latest ideas to a committee, do you think it would be a good idea to discuss them with some of the more influential members before the presentation?

Is that manipulative or skilful? It's all a question of perception.

OUR CHALLENGE

To have our antennae tuned into the right frequencies and to be able to navigate the political waters, many of which may be infested by sharks.

IT'S NOT ME – IT'S THEM!

Many people in organisations believe that politics is used by others for their own benefit. It is very rare for people to admit to being a 'politician' or to be proud of it.

You may say, 'It is other people who are political but not me'.

BUT...

They may be saying exactly the same thing about you!

It is our interpretation of other people's behaviour and their interpretation of ours that will determine how political you are.

INTRODUCTION

> *If you really want an organisation to achieve success in today's complex environment, you cannot afford to turn a blind eye to the political dimension of your business or service.*

This quote from Sir David Varney, Chairman of the Leading with Political Awareness Steering Board, appears in the report 'Leading with political intelligence' written by Professor Jean Hartley and colleagues and published by the Chartered Management Institute.

WHAT POLITICAL ANIMAL ARE YOU?

HOW DO YOU MEASURE UP?

The key question to ask yourself is, 'What political animal am I?' One of the ways to find out is to measure yourself against two important criteria:

1. Your **goal alignment** – to what extent do you work towards your own goals or do you put energy and effort into working towards the goals of the organisation AND your own goals?

2. To what extent are you **politically intelligent**? In other words are you able to:
    - Read what is happening in the organisation at a time when everything is changing?
    - Understand how decisions are really made?
    - Use different types of power at different times with different people?
    - Know who are the key individuals in the organisation?
    - Know who and how to influence to get your ideas accepted?
    - Understand where different types of power are and how it moves over time?
    - Be clear about the different agendas that exist in the organisation?
    - Demonstrate similar skills to those of a chess player – thinking ahead of the many different moves and possible responses?

WHAT POLITICAL ANIMAL ARE YOU?

THE ANIMAL MODEL

If the two criteria of political intelligence and goal alignment are plotted against each other, the result is four distinct 'political animals':

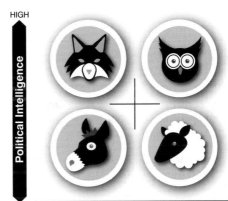

HIGH

Political Intelligence

LOW ◄ **Goal Alignment with Organisation** ► HIGH

ANIMAL CHARACTERISTICS

Each of the four animals have very different positive and negative characteristics:

FOXES

- Clever
- Cunning
- Adaptable
- Resourceful
- Sly
- Kill for fun
- Furry!

OWLS

- Observant
- Kill for food
- Swift
- Silent
- Aloof and distant
- Wise
- Feathery!

ANIMAL CHARACTERISTICS

MULES

- Determined
- Hard working
- Noisy
- Bad tempered
- Heavy load carrier
- A plodder but sure-footed
- Hairy!

SHEEP

- Trusting
- Innocent
- Naïve
- Follower
- Gentle and timid
- Loyal
- Woolly!

In reality you may be a little bit of all these animals at different times. It is also important to note that none of them is 'right'. You need to make decisions about what animal you would like to be at any given time.

FOXES ARE **CLEVER**

These people have high political intelligence and use it primarily in pursuit of their personal goals.

Clever characters are individuals who understand the political climate and are aware not only of the written rules but also of the unwritten ones, the ways to get things done both formally and informally. They may use this knowledge for personal gain, and may be skilful at placing blame and/or responsibility onto others.
They may be seen as playing games, often with a concealed motivation.

WHAT POLITICAL ANIMAL ARE YOU?

OWLS ARE **WISE**

These people have high political intelligence and typically this is used to align their personal goals with those of the organisation. (They believe time, effort and energy are wasted if goal alignment does not occur.)

Wise people know and understand the politics of the organisation. They, like the clever group, know how to manoeuvre around organisational procedures when required and do so by revealing their motivation to others so they are not misunderstood. They work in ways that are beneficial both to the organisation and themselves. They are unlikely to undertake activities solely in pursuit of their own interests.

WHAT POLITICAL ANIMAL ARE YOU?

SHEEP ARE **TRUSTING**

These people have low levels of political intelligence and are concerned to meet both the organisation's goals and their own.

Innocents tend to be suspicious of the whole issue of politics. This may be because they link political intelligence with Fox-like behaviour – associating with the negative aspects rather than the positive behaviour of the Owls. For others, politics is a game that must be avoided, either consciously or unconsciously.

They pursue the organisational goals and their own simultaneously. They tend to be innocent in terms of their blindness to power and organisational decision-making processes.

WHAT POLITICAL ANIMAL ARE YOU?

MULES ARE **DETERMINED**

These individuals have low levels of political intelligence and put their energy into the pursuit of their own goals.

People in this quadrant can be unaware of the formal and informal power structures, and are primarily concerned with achieving their own goals. They tend to be determined individuals who stick resolutely to their plans. They are convinced that they are right and are not afraid of telling others, whether it is appropriate or not.

WHAT POLITICAL ANIMAL ARE YOU?

FOX OR OWL? SHEEP OR MULE?

In organisational life it can be fairly easy to recognise the four types.

Sometimes people are a combination of the different animals and therefore are more difficult to identify.

You now need to consider what type of animal you might be, and do the same for those individuals who are important to you in the organisation.

Where would you put yourself on the animal grid? Where would you put some of your colleagues? Write the initials of key colleagues in the appropriate quadrant of the model. What type of animal would you like to be?

WHAT POLITICAL ANIMAL ARE YOU?

UNDERSTAND WHO HAS POWER

An important aspect of the animal model is that you probably started your organisational career somewhere near the 'low political intelligence' end of the graph. During the early stages of your working life you may have started to realise the need to understand how the organisation **really** works.

For example, the most powerful person in the organisation is normally the person with the most positional power – eg the managing director, CEO or head of the department or division.

The critical question is, who is the second most powerful? It is likely to be somebody who does not have a senior position but has **proxy power** – ie they 'borrow' it from another person who is powerful. In many organisations it is the secretary or PA of the MD/CEO who has a huge amount of power – which is why they are known as 'gatekeepers'. Upset them at your peril!

WHAT POLITICAL ANIMAL ARE YOU?

YOU HAVE A CHOICE

So, you quickly learn in your organisation that it is not a good idea to upset the secretaries or PAs to senior management. But something else also happens at this time that can affect our career opportunities and our lives.

Because most political behaviour in organisations is perceived to be in the negative, many people associate the self-serving foxes with political intelligence and then either consciously or unconsciously say to themselves – 'If that is what being political is, then I don't want anything to do with it'.

The good news: there is an alternative! It is possible to develop political intelligence and, if you choose, to become more owl-like, to work towards the achievement of **both** your own goals and those of the organisation. This is a decision that is very personal to you (you may prefer to be a different animal). What is important is to understand the implication of being perceived as each of the animals.

WHAT POLITICAL ANIMAL ARE YOU?

IDENTIFYING POLITICAL ANIMALS

Each person in your organisation (including you) will subconsciously demonstrate behaviours that are associated with their political animal preference.

Sometimes, however, you will see someone demonstrating conflicting political animal behaviours, and there are usually two reasons for this:

1. They are genuinely trying to develop new political intelligence behaviours, because they recognise that their current preferences are unproductive for their current role.

2. They are deliberately masking their preference in order to get what they want!

In most cases the political behavioural preferences people demonstrate are relatively easy to identify, and the following pages should help you spot a Fox, Owl, Mule or a Sheep!

WHAT POLITICAL ANIMAL ARE YOU?

FOX SPOTTING!

Foxes tend to use body language that masks their thinking. People often think of foxes as being good poker players! Charming and charismatic one minute, they can equally be arrogant and bullying the next.

They know the key decision-makers' 'real' agendas, who is 'in' and who is 'out', where to access information, where the power bases are, and how to utilise the 'unwritten' rules. They know what the 'real' organisational chart looks like within the business and who they need to influence, flatter, hustle or bully in order to get what they want.

They know how to get decisions made outside of the formal organisational channels, are quite happy to break rules to get results, and are often seen as being Machiavellian. Their primary goal is to meet their own objectives, which can be to the detriment of others achieving their goals and objectives. For them, it's nothing personal – it's just business.

WHAT POLITICAL ANIMAL ARE YOU?

OWL SPOTTING!

Owls are proactive in aligning their goals and objectives to those of the organisation. They have a high degree of emotional intelligence, are empathetic and understand the feelings, desires, hopes and aspirations of others and seek ways to achieve win-win outcomes. For them 'compromise' is not a dirty word but a good result.

They are tough on facts about under-performance, even in themselves, but they are equally open-minded as to the reasons and see the disclosure of personal development needs as a strength – not a weakness. They are happy to move people on if that is good for the organisation, because they know that in the long-run it will be best for the individual as well.

They tend to be transparent in their thought and influencing processes, and are consistent in their behaviour and approach towards different people. They are tactful, respectful and know when to speak and when to remain quiet. They keep confidences and develop respect and loyalty in people through their own example of good practice.

WHAT POLITICAL ANIMAL ARE YOU?

SHEEP SPOTTING!

Sheep are loyal to the organisation but can appear naïve. You will often hear them say things like 'it's not fair', when referring to situations where a more skilful political operator has outmanoeuvred them.

They tend to have a small and select network of colleagues who they meet and 'bleat' with regularly over a coffee or at the water cooler! They often demonstrate more passive behaviours than the other types of animals. They can be flexible, supportive and empathetic in their approach towards work and others.

Sheep usually have the best interest of the organisation and other people at heart, but play by the formal 'written' rules, often remaining unaware of the 'unwritten' ones and how they can be used to generate positive results. They tend to believe that the formal organisational chart represents where the decision-making and power reside within the organisation.

WHAT POLITICAL ANIMAL ARE YOU?

MULE SPOTTING!

Mules are determined, forthright and vocal, often offering their personal opinions in inappropriate places. They are stubborn and often hard working people who can be seen by others as being inflexible. They generally work towards the achievement of their own personal goals.

They can be impatient of others, dislike changes to their routine or having to learn new things. They can appear to enjoy finding fault in things, but will rarely offer alternative solutions to resolve problems.

Mules make statements such as, 'We tried that 20 years ago. It didn't work then and it won't work now.' Typically they have a 'not invented here' mentality towards new ideas, systems, services, products and processes. They will be the people at meetings or at the water cooler challenging the wisdom of others: 'He doesn't know anything about...'

WHAT POLITICAL ANIMAL ARE YOU?

HOW THE ANIMALS BEHAVE

How might each of the animals deal with the four scenarios at the start of this book?
Here are some examples for you to consider:

Scenario One - A COMMON TALE OF EMAIL ABUSE (see page 9)

Fox: Would seek to blame and to show that it is not their fault. Their email response, copied to all, would say: 'I have been very busy with more important work. I cannot respond to the needs of your department particularly when you were not clear on the deadline.'

Mule: Attack may be the best form of defence. Their email, copied to all, might say: 'I am busy and you didn't provide me with xyz last week either.'

Sheep: Their email, probably not copied, would state: 'I am so sorry, I completely forgot. I will stop what I am doing right now and get you the information ASAP.'

Owl: Their email, possibly copied to all, may say: 'I recognise your concerns and I share these. This has been an oversight on my part for which I apologise. In the future it would be useful for me to have a clearer deadline from you so that I can plan my workload better and then we can all work together more effectively.'

HOW THE ANIMALS BEHAVE

Scenario Two - THE CLOSED DOOR (see page 10)

Fox: Will not accept the reasons given and will use their extensive network to find out the real reason. This will probably be done without the manager's knowledge, with pressure put on others to divulge information. They will persist until they have the information. If it is not forthcoming they will make this an excuse not to co-operate with others in the future.

Mule: 'This is outrageous and completely against company policy. I am going to HR immediately to put in a formal complaint against you and your boss.'

Sheep: 'OK – it's not a problem. I fully understand and I will wait for the next opportunity.'

Owl: 'OK – I can sense this is not the right time, thanks for the advice, I appreciate you being clear with me.' Afterwards will choose a good time and ask questions like:

- Can you let me know when the time is right to discuss this with you?
- Do you have any ideas on how I can understand better why I wasn't successful?
- Did your boss say why I was not to ask any questions?
- Regarding the next opportunity, what do I now have to do, perhaps differently, to make sure I am successful?

(39)

HOW THE ANIMALS BEHAVE

Scenario Three - THE GOAL DIFFERENCE (see page 11)

Fox: Does nothing. Taking no action ensures that the personal goals of both people are met. Not good for the organisation though.

Mule: Will ensure that somebody at a high level knows what is happening. Action will then be taken, putting the manager in a difficult position. When the mule suffers from a worsening relationship with their manager they will say, 'Nothing to do with me – it's their fault'.

Sheep: May not take any action at all, fearing reprisals from their manager. The outcome however is a massive reduction in the level of trust between them and the sheep will complain behind the scenes (probably to other sheep) about, 'The boss being political and only thinking of their own goals'.

Owl: Will be concerned that the organisation is not benefiting. Action taken will be to decide if this is a battle worth fighting. If it is they may wait for a better time to discuss it with the manager and will be empathetic with their situation. It may be possible to bring in other objectives or information to influence the manager to refer the matter to others. The owl will also help the manager to understand the implications of their behaviour when others find out what they have done.

HOW THE ANIMALS BEHAVE

Scenario Four - ROCK AND A HARD PLACE (see page 12)

Fox: Delegates to a member of the team. Does whatever it takes to be taken out of the firing line and sets another up for failure as the personal risk is too high. Positions the presentation as a development opportunity for one of their team.

Mule: Gives the presentation themselves, making it very clear that they do not really support it but are undertaking the task at their manager's request. 'Quite honestly I have to do this because I have been asked to but I don't think it is really an option for this part of the business.'

Sheep: Will worry continually about the friction, discuss with other sheep and then make the presentation and put themselves at the mercy of local management. Will wonder afterwards why they had such a hard time and their reputation has suffered.

Owl: Will know how to reconcile two different agendas. This may involve speaking to an ally of their local CEO to discuss what the presentation will be about and to ensure the local CEO has advance warning of what is going to happen. The content may be amended to ensure local issues are brought into the presentation, ones that the local management support.

PREPARATION IS KEY TO SUCCESS

In organisational life you rarely have a
choice about who you work with. You are
likely to have regular contact with all four
political types. Many people find working with
foxes to be a real challenge. Of course you
don't have to become a fox as well...Owls have
just as much political intelligence, so you do have a
choice about what type of political animal you
want to become.

When you have to interact with foxes you need
to be wary, particularly if you have sheep or
mule tendencies. What follows is a
checklist of questions that will help you
to think through and prepare yourself to
be even more successful.

WORKING WITH FOXES: CHECKLIST

What is the issue/situation?

- In the overall scheme of things how important is this to me?
- What is really going on?
- What might be the real agenda?
- Why am I really concerned?
- What is the worst that could happen?
- How long has this been going on?

Who is involved?

- Who else will be affected by the activity/outcome?
- Do I fully understand all the people ramifications?
- How might others react if I do something/nothing?
- Has anyone else had this problem in the past?
- Who else do I need to involve?
- Where are my allies who can give me more insight into what is happening?
- Whose support do I need to get?

WHAT POLITICAL ANIMAL ARE YOU?

WORKING WITH FOXES: CHECKLIST

What do I know about the other party?

- Is it me, my position or my boss they are working against?
- What are they really motivated by?
- What evidence do I have?
- How can I confirm my suspicions?
- What might be driving their behaviour?
- Is there a hidden agenda?
- Are they working to their own or the organisation's objectives?
- How much support do they have: a lot or only a little? And who?
- Have they done this to someone else before?
- Do I like them?

Am I part of the problem?

- Am I seen as a soft touch or too nice?
- Am I difficult to deal with?
- Have my motives or behaviour been misunderstood?
- Could it be revenge for something I once did?
- Have I been associated with someone else who is the real target?
- Do I communicate effectively with them?
- How effective am I at influencing?

WHAT POLITICAL ANIMAL ARE YOU?

WORKING WITH FOXES: CHECKLIST

What should my strategy be?

- Am I really sure there is a need to do something?
- How will I go about it?
- Is there a sequence to be followed?
- How soon do I need to start?
- Should I approach them directly, or work with/through others?
- Who do I need to alert/get onside/build alliances with?
- Are there alternative approaches that are less risky?

WHAT POLITICAL ANIMAL ARE YOU?

NOW YOU'RE READY TO MOVE ON

Having understood the characteristics of
the different types of political animal, and
identified your current profile, it is time to
consider what type of political animal you
would like to be.

What might you have to do to become
more politically intelligent? The following
sections will show you the skills you
need to move 'up' the Animal model
axis – it is up to you to decide
whose goals are more
important to you – yours
or the organisation's…or
both!.

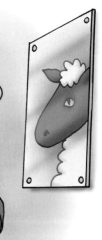

POLITICAL INTELLIGENCE
SKILL DEVELOPMENT

POLITICAL INTELLIGENCE SKILL DEVELOPMENT

EVERYONE GAINS

People are not born with political intelligence; they develop the skill over time as a result of being exposed to different organisational cultures, working challenges and work colleagues.

Political intelligence is, therefore, a skill that can be developed by anyone. When applied in a positive way, the skills of political intelligence can help people achieve not only their own goals and those of others, but also those of the organisation – so that everyone gains positively (emotionally and materially) from the experience.

When applied regularly in your daily working practices, the following practical tips will help you to become more 'positively' politically astute in your workplace.

POLITICAL INTELLIGENCE SKILL DEVELOPMENT

FOUR KEY SKILLS

The key skills of political intelligence can be divided into four distinct areas:

1. Communication
2. Influencing
3. Networking
4. Factor X

Factor X is the final, critical area that provides the difference that makes the difference!

In each area there are 10 tips for you to implement at your workplace.

FACTOR

X

POLITICAL INTELLIGENCE SKILL DEVELOPMENT

SKILL 1: COMMUNICATION
TOP TIPS

Tip 1 Practise being open and honest about what you want to achieve and how you want to go about achieving it, as this creates trust. Effective relationships are built on trust. Trust gives you allies and allies give you positive power and influence.

Tip 2 If you cannot be open and honest with others, don't lie to them (people have long memories). Consider instead being open and honest about the fact you cannot be open and honest at this particular time!

> *(Sometimes)* ❛ *It is better to say nothing and be thought a fool, than to say something and remove all doubt* ❜
>
> Abraham Lincoln

POLITICAL INTELLIGENCE SKILL DEVELOPMENT

SKILL 1: COMMUNICATION

TOP TIPS

Tip 3 'Conversation' is when two people are talking but no one is listening! 'Dialogue' is when one person is talking and the other person is genuinely listening. Practise improving your dialogue skills by improving your 'active' listening skills. You have two ears and one mouth – use them in that ratio.

Tip 4 Practise demonstrating 'understanding' by summarising (in a bullet point form) the key points of a dialogue you have with someone. Do the same at meetings by summarising the key points that were discussed and the actions people will take.

Tip 5 If you are asked a question and do not know the answer, admit you do not know and say you will find out and get back to them as soon as you can. Then do just that!

Tip 6 Regularly invite feedback from colleagues and customers on your work performance. Do not see feedback as criticism or an attack on your personality!

POLITICAL INTELLIGENCE SKILL DEVELOPMENT

SKILL 1: COMMUNICATION
TOP TIPS

Tip 7 Really listen to feedback that is given, ask questions to gain clarity on exactly what the person means, and thank them. After receiving feedback, reflect on whether or not it is relevant. If it is, decide what practical things you can do to use the feedback in your daily working practices.

Tip 8 When faced with someone who disagrees with your point of view, try not to get defensive. Practise the skill of seeing arguments from the other person's perspective, gain clarity on their position by asking them open and probing questions – but not in a way that makes the person feel you are simply interrogating them.

Tip 9 Communicate to others your objectives and meet with your key stakeholders (those who have an interest in your success) to discuss their objectives.

Tip 10 Active listening is the key to effective communication. The questionnaire on the following pages will help you identify your communication strengths and weaknesses.

SKILL 1: COMMUNICATION
ACTIVE LISTENING QUESTIONNAIRE

Others may judge your motives by the way in which you communicate – are you a good listener or just interested in your own agenda? This is the difference between Owl and Fox behaviour. Most of us have communication weaknesses. Consider your answers to these questions and those on the next page:

Selective listening	Yes	No
Are there some individuals you avoid having to listen to?		
Are there certain categories of people you find difficult to listen to?		
Would someone's appearance prejudice you so that you could not listen objectively?		
Might a person's accent or way of speaking make him/her not worth listening to?		
Do you 'tune out' on certain topics?		
Do you refuse to listen to things that may make you feel uncomfortable?		
Do you pay attention only to the good things (or only to the bad things) you hear?		
Do you listen chiefly for facts and overlook expressions of feeling, opinion or prejudice?		
Do you listen purely for your own purposes without thinking what the other person needs?		

POLITICAL INTELLIGENCE SKILL DEVELOPMENT

SKILL 1: COMMUNICATION
ACTIVE LISTENING QUESTIONNAIRE

Attention	Yes	No
Do you let your mind wander or pursue thoughts of your own?		
Do you spend most of the time thinking what you are going to say next?		
Are you easily distracted by other things going on around you?		
Do you have ways of kidding the speaker you are paying attention when you are not?		
Does your body language (wandering gaze, stifled yawn, tapping foot, or drumming fingers) ever reveal that you are getting bored, impatient or irritable?		

Interruptions	Yes	No
Are you always ready to jump in with your own ideas as soon as the other person pauses?		
If the other person says something you disagree with do you interrupt to put your point of view?		
If you can guess the end of a person's sentence, do you complete it for him/her?		
If so, do you then continue talking yourself? Do you try to stop the speaker if you feel he or she is getting angry or upset?		

Which is your worst communication challenge? Work on it now!

POLITICAL INTELLIGENCE SKILL DEVELOPMENT

SKILL 2: INFLUENCING

TOP TIPS

Tip 1 Learn the difference between passive, aggressive and assertive behaviours. Passive and aggressive behaviours are likely to result in you losing, or winning by making the other party lose. Assertiveness ensures that you both win. When you work together again you will both look forward to it because the outcome was successful last time!

Tip 2 When you promise to do something for a colleague or a customer, follow it through and deliver what you promised – both customers and colleagues have very long memories.

Tip 3 Understand that 'power' does not necessarily equate to how high someone is in an organisational hierarchy. For example, the personal assistant to a CEO is usually on a low salary grade, but has power to influence the CEO's thinking (normally in a subtle way) that is disproportionate to their actual place in the hierarchy!

POLITICAL INTELLIGENCE SKILL DEVELOPMENT

SKILL 2: INFLUENCING

TOP TIPS

Tip 4 Be aware that your organisational chart does not reflect where the true decision-making authority resides within your organisation. Create your own 'political' chart showing who you need to influence in order to reach the key decision-makers.

Tip 5 Practise conducting a stakeholder analysis so that you understand not only who your key stakeholders are but, more importantly, what they need from you and how they will measure the success of those needs being met. Always show key stakeholders your analysis and invite them to give you feedback on your assumptions.

Tip 6 When proposing at a meeting something important that you want accepted or implemented, ensure you have 'sold' your idea and have the support of the key decision-makers who can influence the outcome. Consider doing this prior to the meeting taking place.

POLITICAL INTELLIGENCE SKILL DEVELOPMENT

SKILL 2: INFLUENCING

TOP TIPS

Tip 7 Identify the types of political animal that exist in your organisation and tailor your approach towards them.

Tip 8 When you disagree with a colleague on a subject, do not get defensive. Instead be honest about the 'real' reasons for your objection – especially if you feel personal values, beliefs or cultural norms are not being taken into account. Then work with the colleague to overcome your objections and find an acceptable compromise.

Tip 9 Fully understand other people's positions before stating your own – they will then believe that you are interested in them and their agenda. This can be done by asking a series of open, probing and clarifying questions.

Tip 10 Develop a process for influencing – see next page.

POLITICAL INTELLIGENCE SKILL DEVELOPMENT

SKILL 2: INFLUENCING

A PROCESS FOR INFLUENCING

One definition of influence is, 'getting others to *want* to do what you want them to do'. Others might say it is more a question of using assertive behaviours that are closer to persuasion than influence.

The owl politician will have recognised the value in setting win/win outcomes as the goal when influencing because it retains goodwill and positive relationships for the future. This does not happen by chance.

Influencing is a five-stage process:
1. Establish your goals and priorities.
2. Identify the nature of your relationship.
3. Identify your resources.
4. Understand the other person's situation.
5. Reach agreement.

POLITICAL INTELLIGENCE SKILL DEVELOPMENT

SKILL 2: INFLUENCING
A PROCESS FOR INFLUENCING

Stage one requires you to be very clear about what you want to achieve from the outset. In true objective-setting terms, the need to be specific, to have a timeframe and to be realistic about the probability of success are all essential elements to be clear on. Without this clarity it is easy to embark on a futile effort that wastes time and may cause friction with others, or worse. Sometimes when you establish clarity you may decide not to try to influence as it may be the wrong time or place etc.

Stage two recognises the importance of the quality of the relationship. It is much easier to influence someone with whom you have rapport. This rapport can come from putting yourself in the other person's shoes, recognising their motivations and concerns, and behaving in a way they recognise. This may mean flexing your personal style to match theirs.

SKILL 2: INFLUENCING

A PROCESS FOR INFLUENCING

Stage three is about generating support. It is the point at which having a good network becomes extremely useful and the reason why effective organisational politicians invest time in developing one. By accessing colleagues, either your own or those of the person to be influenced, it may well be possible indirectly to shift the thinking in the direction you want. The word ally is used deliberately to describe the other party. This helps you to think positively about the person you are seeking to influence. It is too easy to think of others as adversaries or enemies.

Stage four is about identifying the power and resources at your disposal as a consequence of the position you hold, the skills you command, the people you know, the information you possess etc. Your bargaining powers will be far greater than you imagine.

POLITICAL INTELLIGENCE SKILL DEVELOPMENT

SKILL 2: INFLUENCING
A PROCESS FOR INFLUENCING

Stage five is about making it happen. It is quite common to have covered all the previous four stages and still fall at the final hurdle. Key to stage five is aiming, at all costs, for a win/win outcome. Many people see no difference between this and a compromise. The difference is that a compromise (often the product of a 'split the difference' type of conversation) leaves neither party totally happy – indeed they feel compromised. On the next occasion they may not be so co-operative.

Sometimes the gap between the two parties seems too big to allow agreement. This is when the importance of the first four stages becomes clear. If sufficient attention to each stage has been given, there will invariably be an alternative win/win outcome that can be accomplished. This will only be achieved if the relationship, the understanding of each other's position, the positive mindset and the flexibility to consider all the options are brought together successfully. The ability to communicate well is absolutely critical to this process.

POLITICAL INTELLIGENCE SKILL DEVELOPMENT

SKILL 3: NETWORKING

TOP TIPS

Tip 1 Identify the 'opinion formers' in the organisation – get close to them, observe their behaviours and techniques and learn how they network and influence so effectively.

Tip 2 Recognise other people's successes – send congratulatory notes or emails (but be careful not to appear patronising).

Tip 3 Make allies and build informal relationships with people who are 'well connected'. For example, the coffee shop assistant probably hears more in a day than you do in a month!

Tip 4 Don't spread yourself too thinly. Having too many people in your network is exhausting. Go for quality and appropriateness and not simply quantity. Make a habit of regularly reviewing your network. Who else should you be in contact with? Are you seeing the same chosen few to the exclusion of others?

Tip 5 Write articles for the organisational newsletter or institute magazine etc.

POLITICAL INTELLIGENCE SKILL DEVELOPMENT

SKILL 3: NETWORKING

TOP TIPS

Tip 6 Volunteer, set up or offer to lead new and challenging projects or committees.

Tip 7 Join societies that are not linked to your work (eg Round Table, sports clubs etc) and organisations that are (eg professional institute, trade association etc).

Tip 8 Value diversity in your workplace. Build relationships with people who have different views, perspectives, cultures and experiences to your own. Get involved in benchmarking, community projects etc – any activity that will enable you to make new contacts in other organisations.

Tip 9 Categorise your contacts into those who provide *influence*, *information* or *expertise*. Is there one category that is in imbalance or missing?

Tip 10 Learn the art of networking – see next page.

SKILL 3: NETWORKING
DEVELOPING YOUR NETWORK

The art of networking
It has never been more true, in the modern organisation *who you know* can often be as important as *what you know*. In the world of politics with a big P you will rarely see a successful player who is not very well connected. It is no different in organisations.

Quality versus quantity
Some people find it quite a challenge to take the initiative in making and meeting new contacts. Others have too many. It is possible to have so many people in your network that you don't have a meaningful relationship with any of them. Or, of course, it could be that you know a lot of people – but not the right ones! Only you can determine who is right for your own situation.

Intelligence
For you to fulfil your job effectively you need to have the right information at the right time. This you can get by developing your own network rather than relying on your organisation's formal communications systems. These systems are often inefficient and, in the worst cases, have been infiltrated by politicians with their own agendas.

POLITICAL INTELLIGENCE SKILL DEVELOPMENT

SKILL 3: NETWORKING
DEVELOPING YOUR NETWORK

Make a list of all of your contacts (people who do not say 'who?' when you call).

- Are there any important omissions?
- Are you in danger of neglecting some of them?
- Are you giving as well as receiving?
- Are you seeing too much of the people you like?
- Is your network too wide?
- Do you have too many people or not enough?
- Do they tend to be all from one organisation or section?
- Are they of sufficient quality?
- Can they give you access to high quality information?
- Are there people from whom you can access more power?

POLITICAL INTELLIGENCE SKILL DEVELOPMENT

SKILL 4: FACTOR X

TOP TIPS

Tip 1 Choose the 'right' battleground to make a stand because you don't have to win every time. Strive to achieve win/win or compromise outcomes and demonstrate flexibility.

Tip 2 Practise framing any negative (developmental) feedback that you need to give in a positive (motivational way). People, like you, will always make mistakes; hitting them over the head when they know they have underperformed is counter-productive. Adopt a coaching, as opposed to a 'telling' approach, when giving feedback.

Tip 3 Timing is everything. Would you ask a pilot to talk about their love of flying just as they were about to land a plane! Be aware of the pressures, needs and challenges that your colleagues face so you can choose the right moment to speak with them.

Tip 4 There are morning people and evening people – which type is your boss? Approach them at the right time of day.

Tip 5 Avoid getting involved in inappropriate conversations or deliberately offending other people. Humour that seeks to demean or humiliate others is never acceptable at work.

SKILL 4: FACTOR X

TOP TIPS

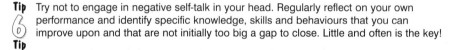

Tip 6 Try not to engage in negative self-talk in your head. Regularly reflect on your own performance and identify specific knowledge, skills and behaviours that you can improve upon and that are not initially too big a gap to close. Little and often is the key!

Tip 7 Never try to 'win' at the expense of others losing or betraying a relationship.

Tip 8 Keep current in your own area of professional practice and be seen as a 'thought leader' for a specialised subject in your field. Because information is power, become a knowledge sharing bee – and not a knowledge hoarding monster!

Tip 9 Avoid gossiping with colleagues and customers because it reduces your credibility, can be hurtful to others, creates enemies, will label you as a time waster and make people suspicious of your motives.

Tip 10 Finally, develop your skills in the areas of power and influence (see next page).

SKILL 4: FACTOR X

POWER AND INFLUENCE

When people are asked if they would like to have more power, many say 'no'.

When they are asked if they would like to be more influential, most say 'yes'.

The link between the two is that more power will typically give you more influence – but how do you build the right sort of power that you will be comfortable using?

POLITICAL INTELLIGENCE SKILL DEVELOPMENT

SKILL 4: FACTOR X

DIFFERENT TYPES OF POWER

There are many different types of power, some given to us by position and some that can be developed. Some types of power you may be comfortable using; some you may not. Consider the following checklist of types of power – which ones do you think you have?

	Yes	No
Resource power – People do as I want because I have or control resources they value.		
Information power – I can influence the behaviour of others because I have access to information that they need or desire.		
Position (or legitimate) power – I have power over others because I hold a powerful position in the social or business hierarchy. My invisible label says, 'I'm in charge'.		
Proxy power – I have influence because I am connected to powerful people.		
Reward power – People do as I want because I can reward those who comply.		
Expert power – People do as I require because they respect my knowledge and expertise.		
Sanctions power – People do as I require because I can punish those who don't.		

Continued…..

POLITICAL INTELLIGENCE SKILL DEVELOPMENT

SKILL 4: FACTOR X
DIFFERENT TYPES OF POWER

	Yes	No
Personal (or referent) power – People do as I wish because they like me.		
Status power – People do as I wish because I have status in the group. I may be the oldest, the longest serving, the only one with a degree or whatever.		
Charisma power – People do as I wish because they respond to my personality, vision, enthusiasm and/or charm.		
Favour power – People do as I wish because I build a bank balance of favours and look for favours in return when I need them.		
Technical power – People do as I wish because I know how to influence behaviour and apply my knowledge with skill.		
Social power – I have influence because I have high social skills, am able to read others' motives and/or have an ability to diffuse conflict.		
Success power – I influence others because I have a reputation for achieving objectives, exceeding targets and generally doing well at my chosen role.		

SKILL 4: FACTOR X

DIFFERENT TYPES OF POWER

Some questions for you to think about:

- Did you realise that there are so many different types of power?
- Do you have more or less power than you thought?
- Which of these sources of power do you use most frequently?
- Which do you not use at all?
- Which ones do you like using?
- Which ones do you not like using?
- Which would you like to have more of?
- How might you get more?

POLITICAL INTELLIGENCE SKILL DEVELOPMENT

SKILL 4: FACTOR X
DIFFERENT TYPES OF POWER

Tip: information power can give you much influence. Consider people in your organisation who are well placed to help you with what is really happening in the organisation. They are normally not very senior people and can include:

- Secretaries and PAs
- Chauffeurs
- Cleaners
- People who work in the staff restaurant or canteen
- In the case of one large broadcaster, it is the car park security guard!

Never, ever confuse titles with power!

Example: the lead character's reply to his son in the Woody Allen movie Mighty Aphrodite, when asked who the boss is between Mummy and Daddy, was: 'Who is the boss? You have to ask that? I'm the boss. Mummy is only the decision-maker'.

Titles can be deceiving.

POLITICAL INTELLIGENCE SKILL DEVELOPMENT

SKILL 4: FACTOR X

IDEAS FOR DEVELOPING MORE POWER

- Become known as a subject matter expert to whom people come for your expertise. This may need you to be more open about your capabilities

- Be over generous in doing favours for people when they ask and do not be afraid to ask for that favour in return. Build a strong credit balance – it will provide you with interest!

- Learn to reference work from outside of the organisation – 'In xyz company they do this', or ' I was at a conference last week hosted by xyz and they stated that….' This comes with much more credibility (unfortunately) than you quoting it for yourself

SKILL 4: FACTOR X

IDEAS FOR DEVELOPING MORE POWER

- Be generous with your rewards – develop a name for yourself for congratulating and thanking people for their efforts or good work done

- Many people don't believe that they have charisma power, yet all of us have it in different ways – so use it!

- Feedback indicates that people are not comfortable using or having sanctions power, yet many of us have it (whether we like it or not) as a consequence of our position or status

POLITICAL
INTELLIGENCE TOOLS

POLITICAL INTELLIGENCE TOOLS

KEY TO POLITICAL INTELLIGENCE

How can you actively manage the image you want to create? How can you make sure that others are left with the perception that you want? How can you ensure that your behaviour will be interpreted as owl and not fox?

Reveal and Ask is a fabulous technique that will help enormously.

In order not to be misunderstood when communicating – in particular when asking questions, the intention of which can often be misunderstood – it is critical to balance Ask with Reveal.

Reveal is as simple as explaining your reasoning, where you are coming from or your intention for asking the question.

In our busy lives and working environments the tendency for us all is to use more Ask than Reveal. Using more Ask confuses people!

POLITICAL INTELLIGENCE TOOLS

KEY TO POLITICAL INTELLIGENCE

Example: The question to a teenager such as, 'Where have you been?' will most likely generate a defensive or aggressive response and possibly cause relationship difficulties. However, disclosing why you are asking the question may well lead to a more productive conversation.

Example: In the workplace when your boss says, 'Are you busy?' your mind may race with thoughts such as: 'Why the question? Could it be more work coming my way? Is it because that report is a little late? Or is it genuine curiosity?' This in turn may make you defensive, inaccurate, misleading or even untruthful!

The boss could improve the quality of response by revealing, before asking, the reasoning behind the question.

Are you busy?

POLITICAL INTELLIGENCE TOOLS

KEY TO POLITICAL INTELLIGENCE

Ways to improve Reveal – make your thinking process visible:

What to do	What to say
Talk about any assumptions you are making and any information you may have that others don't.	*'I have made an assumption. Can I check this with you? I made this assumption based on…'*
Be clear as to how you have reached any conclusions (normally we do this subconsciously), who has been involved or affected and why.	*'I have come to a conclusion and I'd like to tell you what it is.'*
Provide examples to bring your thinking to life.	*'To help us both understand what this may be like, for me it is the same as when I go into a hotel and the receptionist says…'*
When you are disclosing, be more empathetic with the other person. How will they see what you are saying from their perspective?	*'This is what I think and I can imagine that from your point of view this means…'*

KEY TO POLITICAL INTELLIGENCE

Ways to improve Reveal – make your thinking process visible:
Test out with others explicitly your assumptions.

What to do	What to say
Get others to speak openly about your position.	*'What is your view and/or position on what I have said. Do you have any further thoughts? Can you see where I might be going wrong?'*
When people ask questions, you can interpret this in two ways: they are disagreeing with me and testing me out; or they are interested in what I have said and are wanting more information. The second belief will ensure that you respond more positively!	*'That's a really good question and helpful as I haven't thought about that before. That's a good question, can you help me to think through the various options I have?'*
If you are not clear about something then it is better to reveal this than allow an opponent to find it and to make an issue of it.	*'This is the part where I'm not so clear. As you have expertise in this area what are your ideas for …?'*
When 'Revealing' continue to allow others to provide alternatives.	*'What other thoughts do you have, what else have I missed, do you think this will work, do you have any alternatives?'*

POLITICAL INTELLIGENCE TOOLS

KEY TO POLITICAL INTELLIGENCE

Ways to improve Reveal – make your thinking process visible:
Ask **others** to provide information on where they are coming from.

What to do	What to say
Be specific about the information and data base they have.	*'Where does that information come from? Why have you concluded that? Can you tell me, what data do you have for that? From what sources does that come from?'*
Use assertive rather than aggressive language. Learn how they differ.	*Instead of, 'What, you're kidding!' or 'Where's your proof?' say, 'I'm not clear what you are saying, can you tell me the same thing in a slightly different way?'*
Ensure you are clear about their assumptions and reasoning.	*'What has been your thinking that makes you say that? What are the other issues that are linked to this? How is this related to what you said earlier?'*
Explain why you are asking and reveal any emotions behind the question.	*'I'm concerned about xyz. I feel that this would lead to …The reason I'm concerned about this is because…'*
Check your understanding of what is being said.	*'If I said … is that what you mean?'*
And finally…always listen to what is really being said and refrain from thinking about what you are going to say next.	*Repeat back and paraphrase what you think has been said to test your understanding and to show that you are listening and not just interested in your own agenda – as most foxes are!*

Source: The Fifth Discipline Fieldbook by Peter Senge

HOW POLITICAL IS MY ORGANISATION?

THE CAUSES OF POLITICAL BEHAVIOUR

Organisations sometimes put in place policies and procedures that encourage political behaviour – for example, performance management systems with forced distribution, or zero based budgeting systems where business cases have to be made in order to obtain resources or funding. This inevitably means that some people will not be open, will not share information or will protect their own 'turf' at the expense of others.

Whatever is put in place by organisations, however, it is people who choose to behave politically.

Questionnaire

The short questionnaire opposite will help you identify how political your organisation is. When answering, it might be appropriate for you to think about your team, your department, your division or your whole organisation. It is up to you. The scores may be different depending on the area you think about.

Rate each statement as: 3 = very familiar   2 = partly true   1 = rarely applies

HOW POLITICAL IS MY ORGANISATION?

QUESTIONNAIRE

The reorganisation of departments always seem to favour some people over others ☐

Decisions come from nowhere when it is obvious that they have been discussed in secret for months ☐

People often run each other down – but never face-to-face ☐

On occasions you find others have received recognition for what was your hard work ☐

You have the impression that decisions have already been made ahead of the meeting you are attending ☐

Some people seem far more interested in their own goals rather than doing what is best for the organisation ☐

Promotions and pay rises do not always seem to reflect an individual's abilities ☐

Finding out who caused the problem is often more important than looking for the solution ☐

The 'grapevine' frequently seems better informed than the formal communication channels ☐

The external competition hardly seems to get mentioned – our main concern is with internal competition ☐

TOTAL SCORE ☐

HOW POLITICAL IS MY ORGANISATION?

QUESTIONNAIRE: WHAT YOUR SCORE MEANS

A score of 16 and below shows an organisation (or team, department, division etc) with a low negative political environment. So, well done to you as you are part of this environment. It means that your organisation doesn't suffer from negative organisational politics. The sad news is that you are in a minority.

A score of 17 to 23 indicates a moderate level of political behaviour and, therefore, you need to be on your guard to manage this aspect of your organisation. Skill will be required to ensure that productivity, team morale and motivation do not suffer.

A score of 24 and above indicates an organisation with a high level of political activity. It is crucial that you are aware of this and are skilled to manage it. If this is not the case it is your organisation and you that might suffer.

At the time of writing, 5000 people (public, private and voluntary sector employees) have completed this questionnaire and, for all levels of staff, the average median score is 23.

QUESTIONNAIRE: FINDINGS

Looking at the findings from 5000 managers who completed the questionnaire, it is interesting to note:

1. The more senior a person is the lower the score, in general terms. With senior executives it is not unusual for the score to be below 14. This is possibly because they see themselves as non-political.

2. People who have been in an organisation for a relatively short time (less than nine months) have much lower scores than their colleagues in similar roles. This is because they are:

   - Experiencing a honeymoon period
   - Seeing their new organisation through 'rose tinted spectacles'
   - Not seeing political behaviour in colleagues since they don't know them sufficiently well

3. As the questionnaire is completed by different layers of management, the score increases (more political) the more junior the manager.

HOW POLITICAL IS MY ORGANISATION?

INDICATORS OF POLITICAL BEHAVIOUR

- Some individuals seem better informed than others about what's going on
- There is a distinct lack of consistency in the goals and motivations of colleagues
- Some influential senior managers seem to be more interested in their own goals
- Only some successes and some failures get publicised
- Decision-making more often takes place through informal channels
- It appears easier to achieve success by outperforming colleagues than outperforming external competitors
- Certain managers seem to have far more power and influence than their position in the organisational structure would normally suggest

(86) And this is just the tip of the iceberg!

POLITICAL PERCEPTIONS

POLITICAL PERCEPTIONS

FOREWORD

 Whether you think that you can, or that you can't, you are usually right. Henry Ford

- Be ready for your beliefs to be challenged – you have been warned!
- Perceptions of others is a fascinating topic

Consider this common organisational situation:

You are walking along the office corridor, towards colleagues you know well and who are at the water machine, talking to each other. Just as you get to within listening distance they stop talking. How do you interpret their behaviour? Read on…

THE WATER COOLER TALE

It could be they are...

- Talking about me
- Planning a nice surprise for me
- Planning something horrible for me
- Talking about a close friend of mine

- Telling a politically incorrect joke
- Having an affair
- Embarrassed about the subject
- Talking about a secret

... or they have just stopped talking.

Your interpretation of their behaviour will affect your behaviour towards them. If, for instance, you believe they are talking about you, you may become suspicious, concerned, try to find out from colleagues what is going on and be guarded towards them in the future. Consequently, to them you will appear distant or cool, and they will think you are being secretive and not sharing information. Seeing you behave in this way will affect their behaviour towards you.

THE SELF-FULFILLING PROPHECY

You may have heard the expression 'behaviour breeds behaviour'.

This means that if you behave in a certain way towards another person this will in turn affect their behaviour. For example, when you smile at somebody they normally smile back. If you don't smile they probably won't either.

This process is known as the 'self-fulfilling prophecy'. It can work as a negative or positive self-reinforcing cycle.

BELIEFS

You have beliefs about yourself, other people, your organisations, your family and the world/universe etc. These beliefs tend to change over time as you experience the behaviour of others around you.

The beliefs that you hold (sometimes so deep you don't realise that they are there) in turn drive and influence the way you behave towards others.

Example: a homeowner mislays his wallet. He looks everywhere and cannot find it. In the neighbour's back garden he spots a 14 year old youth. The boy appears guilty, furtive, his shoulders are drooped: 'He looks really suspicious… could he, possibly…?'

Soon the man's partner arrives home and presents him with his wallet: 'I found this in my car'. The homeowner looks again at the youth who now suddenly seems just the same as all other young people. Not suspicious at all. 'In fact he's a good lad really! How could I have ever thought such a thing…'

BELIEFS: QUESTIONNAIRE

What you choose to believe about others will influence how you behave towards them. If our homeowner believed that the youth had taken the wallet – what might he have said to him and also, just as important, how might he have said it? It would probably have ended with an argument.

So what are your perceptions about your organisation? Answer the following questionnaire (this page and next). Read each pair of statements and circle either A or B to reflect the way you currently perceive things in your organisation.

A. There are few barriers to effectiveness here.
B. This is not always an easy place to work in.

A. I am always kept informed of what I need to know.
B. I have to work hard to find out what is going on.

A. A lot of healthy debate takes place.
B. A considerable amount of gossiping goes on.

A. Continuous change seems the only way to stay ahead.
B. Changes often seem to be made for the sake of it.

BELIEFS: QUESTIONNAIRE

A. Having lots of contacts makes doing the job much easier.
B. Who you know seems more important than what you know.

A. Promotions and rises are earned the hard way.
B. It pays to keep in with my superiors if I want to get on.

A. Open communications keeps everyone informed.
B. The informal way is the most effective communication channel.

A. Internal competition keeps people performing well.
B. The bonus system often works better for some than others.

A. Consulting widely leads to better outcomes.
B. There is constant manoeuvring in this organisation.

A. The relevant parties are always involved in decisions.
B. Only some individuals seem to be a party to decision-taking.

Total A's [ ]

Total B's [ ]

BELIEFS: QUESTIONNAIRE

So, how many A's did you score and how many B's? Did you notice that the statements tended to describe a similar aspect of organisational life? One statement was negative and one statement was positive.

If you scored more A's than B's this probably means that you tend to see your organisation in a more positive way. It is likely therefore that when you see political behaviour going on you will see the positive aspects. The opposite is true if you scored more B's than A's.

Our beliefs about our organisation and our colleagues will drive our behaviour towards others. What this means in practice is that we need to challenge ourselves with the question: '**Am I seeing what I want to see or what is actually happening?**'

Another challenging question to ask yourself is: 'Am I seeing others as political when they might not be and, in turn, could they be misinterpreting my behaviour?'

WHAT DO YOU SEE?

Do you see an old woman or a young woman?
Look again until you see both of them.

When you saw the young woman were you right?
When you saw the old woman were you right?

There is no right or wrong answer, just different
points of view.

A difference in PERCEPTION!

Leeper's
ambiguous lady

WHAT DO OTHERS SEE?

I see others as political – but how do they see me?

All of us have political tendencies to varying degrees. If others are seeing you as a political animal it becomes important to understand what type of animal that might be as this will affect how others will behave towards you.

How might my behaviour in the organisation be interpreted?

How am I perceived?

One way is to ask trusted colleagues.

POLITICAL PERCEPTIONS

COMMON MISTAKES

- Rejecting political behaviour as being for others
- Failing to understand the political landscape within your workplace
- Misreading the motivations of others
- Enjoying the negative aspects of politics
- Failing to make your intentions clear to others
- Taking your manager's behaviour personally
- Being too subjective

NOTES

CREATING
YOUR MASTER PLAN

CREATING YOUR MASTER PLAN

IMPORTANT QUESTIONS

Now we turn to your political intelligence master plan.

The following grid* contains important questions for you to consider before starting to influence or to interact with a key person in your organisation. Alternatively, use it when things are not going so well. It will prompt you to take action in areas you may have neglected.

Power

Influence	Communication	Networking	Factor 'X'
Who do you think has power and influence in your organisation?	What type of communication is used by the people with power?	How do powerful people network? Where do they go to do it?	Do you choose to ignore certain people who have power?
What type of power is it?	Do people with different power bases communicate differently?	Can you access this place?	What extra power can you borrow, develop or obtain?
Do you have enough power?		Who do you need to network with to give you more power?	What type of power does your boss have and/or use?
What type do you have?	Do you flex your communication style to match other people's styles?	Who do you know with power that you can access?	Have you noticed any 'power shifts' recently?
How can you develop more power and influence?	Do you make it clear to others the power that you have?	Do people with different power bases network differently?	Do you confuse people with power and people with status?
Are you open with others about the types of power you have?			

CREATING YOUR MASTER PLAN

IMPORTANT QUESTIONS

Allies

Influence	Communication	Networking	Factor 'X'
Where and who are your allies who can help you influence others?	Do you understand what processes your allies use to communicate effectively?	Do you know how your allies network and do you observe and replicate their behaviour?	Do you have enough allies?
How can you develop additional relationships that will be useful?	What is it about their communication that makes them effective?	Are you an active member of their network?	Do you know who they are?
Are you overlooking some people who do not hold senior positions?	What types of communication processes do they use, that you could develop?	Do you use their network to gain new allies?	Are there any obvious people who you have overlooked?
Are you overlooking some people who may be close to you?		Where do they go to network?	What about in other organisations?
			What about people in your family and social network?

*The political intelligenceTM diagnostic © 2008 3D Training and Development

CREATING YOUR MASTER PLAN

IMPORTANT QUESTIONS

Agenda

Influence	Communication	Networking	Factor 'X'
Who are the key people and what are their personal and organisational agendas?	How can you communicate more effectively on other people's agendas?	Do you know what the key agendas are for people in your network?	Are you clear as to when and how decisions are made?
How can you influence the agenda of people in power?	How can you link your agenda to the key agendas in the organisation?	How can you find out?	Who might know?
What are currently the most important agendas?	Are you aware of the hidden agendas?	What options exist for you to discover them?	Where are the informal decision points?
Who is interested in your agenda?	Can you read what is not being said?	Do you know if any exist?	Where are the information flows and are you linked into them?
Who do you use to develop your agenda?	Do you link what you say to other people's agendas?	What are the covert personal agendas?	How do you discover information before others?
	Do you recall from previous meetings what the agendas were?	Are there people in your network who know?	

CREATING YOUR MASTER PLAN

IMPORTANT QUESTIONS

Personal style

Influence	Communication	Networking	Factor 'X'
How behaviourally flexible are you when you influence others?	Are you aware of the basic differences in personal styles?	Do you like networking?	Do you volunteer for the right things?
Do you recognise the need to do things differently when dealing with different stakeholders?	Are you able to use more than one?	Are you attending the right functions/activities?	Do you network enough with people who can help you?
Do you deliberately use different approaches when influencing?	Are you aware of your own preference and therefore your own bias?	Are you networked into the right people?	Do you have a diverse group in your network?
Do you know the process of influencing?	Do you use your bias too much?	Do you network too much with people you like?	Do you follow up when networking?
What is your preferred influence style, eg do you persuade, suggest or tell?	Do you tend to use a similar approach when communicating?	Have you ever drawn your own network diagram?	Do you have a positive mindset about behaving flexibly?
Which one works best when?	Do you use appropriate body language?	Is it deep and wide enough?	Do you ask for feedback on your ability to be flexible towards people with different personal styles?
	How can you develop your flexibility of style?	Has it got too many people from one organisation?	
	Who can help you?	Do you network effectively outside of your organisation?	

CREATING YOUR MASTER PLAN

FAQs

Does political behaviour really exist?
It exists because people say it does! Many people experience politics in a range of situations, for instance in the family and socially. There are some organisations where it is less common, according to some people. Ask others, however, and the viewpoint changes.

Why can't there be an organisation where politics is banned?
Whenever people come together they will always be capable of misinterpreting one another's behaviour. Politics is an indisputable facet of human activity. Additionally, organisations are not the rational, logical places that people believe them to be. They are organic, irrational and emotional: decisions get made not because they are the right ones but because somebody is proposing them.

When did it start?
We can point to the earliest manuscripts to show that politics has been with us from the earliest times.

CREATING YOUR MASTER PLAN

FAQs

Other people are political, aren't they?
What is ironic about this question is that the same is being asked about you.

Is politics more common further up the organisation?
Experience and research show that politics is possible of operating at any level. People do have different perceptions, however. Looking 'up' the organisation it is common to hear that people perceive senior managers to be political. The opposite is also true: senior managers look 'down' the organisation and complain about politics getting in the way of implementation.

Is politics more common in larger organisations?
No. Research shows that politics operates in both very small and very large organisations.

(105)

CREATING YOUR MASTER PLAN

FAQs

Is politics used more by men than women?
A very tricky and sensitive question to answer. Research and data to support or deny are thin. It is the author's experience that both genders have the potential to be as political as each other. However, the political behaviour that you observe of both genders may be very different.

You mentioned research – what and where is it?
Director magazine in conjunction with Roffey Park undertook and published reports in November 2002 and 2004. The full reports can be obtained from www.roffeypark.co.uk. Additional research was done in 2007 by Warwick Business School in conjunction with the Chartered Management Institute.

CREATING YOUR MASTER PLAN

FURTHER CONSIDERATIONS

To develop your political intelligence consider:

- What do I need to do differently?
- Who might I go to for help?
- What other resources might I access to help me develop?
- What are the subject areas that I need to work on?
- What am I going to do differently – right now?

> If I am not for myself,
> who will be for me?
> If I am not for others,
> what am I?
> And if not now, when?
>
> Hillel

CREATING YOUR MASTER PLAN

THE 7 LAWS OF POLITICS

1. Politics has been with us since time began (and some might say before!)
2. All of us have political tendencies to varying degrees (and even if you think you don't, this really isn't important as it is how others view you that is crucial).
3. Politics is ever-present in organisations (and it won't go away!)
4. Organisational politics can be a force for good (it can be – honestly!)
5. Individual and organisational goals are not mutually exclusive (why can't we achieve our own goals as well as those of the organisation?)
6. Appropriate responses can reconcile individual, team and organisational needs (you just need to learn how to do this).
7. The appropriate use of politics can get things done in an organisation, for the good of all of us.

Human beings are rational animals Aristotle

People are idiots Dilbert

CREATING YOUR MASTER PLAN

FURTHER DEVELOPMENT OPPORTUNITIES

An in-depth political animal diagnostic, providing you with information on your animal type, is available from the Academy for political intelligence. They can be contacted on + 44 (0) 845 0558927 or www.tafpi.com

A custom designed individual development track, providing invaluable advice on how to become more politically intelligent, is also available from the Academy.

You can also attend the Academy's one-day political intelligence workshop or, if the subject of organisational politics has energised you to develop others, then you can become licensed by the Academy to deliver the workshop to your own clients/colleagues.

For additional resources, downloads, articles, a Q & A area and reference materials visit the Academy's website at www.tafpi.com

REFERENCES AND FURTHER READING

Leading with political awareness,
Warwick Business School, 2007

Politics in organisations,
Holbeche L, Roffey Park Institute, 2002

Office politics: A Survival Guide,
Jane Clarke, Spiro Press, 2001

Psst! Don't tell anyone but... organisational politics is about to go positive,
Bancroft-Turner D and Morley D, Training Journal, 2002

Politics at Work,
Director Magazine, November 2002

Confronting company politics,
Stone B, Palgrave Macmillan,1997

Owl, fox, donkey or sheep: political skills for Managers,
Baddley S and James K, Management Education and Development, Vol.18, part 1,1987

Using Constructive Organisational Politics,
Holbeche L, Roffey Park Institute and Director Magazine, 2004

About the Author

David Bancroft-Turner BA (Hons) MIPD
Dave is the Managing Director of the Academy for political
intelligence. It is dedicated to the promotion of the positive
aspects of organisational politics. The Academy is one of the
country's leading authorities on organisational politics, having
learnt what works and doesn't from a variety of Owls, Foxes,
Sheep and Mules with whom they have worked with over the
past 30 years.

The Academy runs a range of leadership development
programmes all of which contain the 'unwritten rules of leadership'
and how it is done in the real world. The Academy has 70 licensed practitioners
worldwide, qualified to deliver its unique and practical political intelligence programme.

Contact
Dave can be contacted via the Academy for political intelligence
Email: dave@tafpi.com
Phone: +44 (0) 845 0558927 or +44 (0) 1832 272097
www.tafpi.com

ORDER FORM

	No. copies

Your details

Name _____

Position _____

Company _____

Address _____

_____

_____

Telephone _____

Fax _____

E-mail _____

VAT No. (EC companies) _____

Your Order Ref _____

Please send me:

The Workplace Politics _____ Pocketbook ☐

The _____ Pocketbook ☐

The _____ Pocketbook ☐

The _____ Pocketbook ☐

Order by Post
MANAGEMENT POCKETBOOKS LTD
LAUREL HOUSE, STATION APPROACH,
ALRESFORD, HAMPSHIRE SO24 9JH UK

Order by Phone, Fax or Internet
Telephone: +44 (0)1962 735573
Facsimile: +44 (0)1962 733637
E-mail: sales@pocketbook.co.uk
Web: www.pocketbook.co.uk

Customers in USA should contact:
Management Pocketbooks
2427 Bond Street, University Park, IL 60466
Telephone: 866 620 6944   Facsimile: 708 534 7803
E-mail: mp.orders@ware-pak.com
Web: www.managementpocketbooks.com